Sir Isaac Newton

*An Essay on Sir Isaac Newton and Newtonian Thought
as Exemplified in the Stanford Collection of Books,
Manuscripts, and Prints concerning Celestial
Mechanics, Optics, Mathematics, and
Related Disciplines as a History
of Natural Philosophy, by*

FREDERICK E. BRASCH

*Published upon the Occasion of an Exhibition in the
Albert M. Bender Room, The Stanford University Libraries
May 5 through July 30, 1962*

STOCK   Carousel ivory text, 80 lb.
COVER   Beau Brilliant Del Monte red, 65 lb. cover
TYPE   Granjon 11/13
DESIGN   William H. Snyder
PRINTED BY   Stanford University Press

FRONTISPIECE: A stipple after a portrait by Sir Godfrey Kneller painted in 1688, the year following the publication of the first edition of the *Principia*.

ISAACVS NEWTONVS.

FOREWORD

THE FREDERICK E. BRASCH COLLECTION ON SIR ISAAC NEWTON, now comprising some three thousand volumes and many related items, was presented to Stanford University in June, 1941, during the celebration of the University's fiftieth anniversary. The donor and the author of this essay, who is now Curator of the Collection, wished in this way to express his gratitude for the personal interest and kindness and the intellectual stimulus he experienced at Stanford as a special student between 1897 and 1899. Following a distinguished career in the John Crerar Library and the Library of Congress, where for many years he was Chief of the Smithsonian Division, Mr. Brasch returned to Stanford in 1948 to continue the building of the Collection, to prepare a catalog and to advise students and scholars on its use. In the course of time he has become one of the most devoted living authorities on the life and work of Newton and the bibliographical history of his writings. His correspondence on these subjects is world-wide.

Readers of the essay which follows will observe that Mr. Brasch's collecting has not been confined to works "by and about" Newton. He has attempted to build a library which will illuminate Newton's thought by tracing its origins far back into antiquity; and he has brought together the books by Newton's contemporaries which clarify the relationships between his work and that of the great scholars and scientists who were his colleagues, his teachers, and his disciples. He has, moreover, carried Newton's thought down to the present day to show how current scientific concepts are related to and in large part derived from it. The Newton Collection thus forms a coherent and broadly-based research corpus in the history of science which will be of constantly-increasing value to scholars in this and related fields.

Much of the scholarly usefulness and distinction of any great university library consists in special collections which have been built by years of patient, devoted, and expert labor. The Frederick E. Brasch Collection on Sir Isaac Newton may be taken as a classical example of such a resource. In strength and completeness unique in this hemisphere, it is the beloved and absorbing life-work of a true scholar and bibliophile for whom the work has been its own reward. He has received no other save our deep affection and gratitude, and the respect of scholars around the world who have benefited from his wisdom, generosity, and unstinting kindness.

R. C. SWANK
Director of University Libraries

THE SIR ISAAC NEWTON COLLECTION

T WAS IN SEPTEMBER 1895 that the first book relating to Isaac Newton's work was acquired to satisfy a young man's inquiry as to why stars and planets held their places in the heavens, and also the question of why they moved. This little volume, entitled *Steele's Fourteen Weeks Study of Astronomy*, was the original stimulus to a most fascinating and wonderful study in celestial mechanics, the mathematical aspects of the universe and its reality and evolution. It was here that the answers to the above questions on planetary motion were found. It was more particularly the laws of Isaac Newton and those of Johann Kepler, and the analytic treatment of these laws, that were the basis of all my subsequent studies. Through the years, whenever possible, books and pamphlets were acquired, all bearing upon celestial mechanics and especially Newton's life and writings. Today the Isaac Newton Collection at Stanford University contains all the writings of Newton, including the first edition of the *Principia*, which serves as the keystone of the Collection, as well as many editions of the works and commentaries thereon.

This brief introduction presents some of the scientists who, as the creators of the physical sciences, may be called the giants upon whose shoulders Newton stood. This Collection of original treatises and commentaries should form good source material for the history of science generally, as well as the history of special subjects, namely, physics, mathematics, and philosophy. However, it is by no means as complete a collection as we would wish it to be. In addition, the Collection has a considerable number of manuscripts and letters by Newton; a good collection of portrait prints, medallions, and a Wedgwood bas-relief; also a seventeenth century marble bust, a copy possibly of the work of Roubillac or of Rysbrack, two of the most famous sculptors of the period. The works of Newton's contemporaries, such as Edmund Halley, Robert Hooke, Christian Huygens, John Wallis, and many others are also followed by the works of great scholars of the eighteenth century, such as Laplace, d'Alembert, Clairaut, Euler, and so forth. From the United States there are the works of Simon Newcomb, George W. Hill, Ernest W. Brown, Forest R. Moulton, and many others.

THE HERITAGE

The Ancient World

Newton was heir to a great heritage, and the Collection contains many early editions of the writings of the classical Greeks of the Alexandrian school, such as Euclid, Archimedes, Apollonius, and Aristarchus.

The Alexandrian period was the golden age of Greek science. The empirical tendency of all Greek philosophy in the three centuries that followed Aristotle (384–322 B.C.) is a very striking fact, and its association with an increasing skeptical spirit no less so. The greatness of the Alexandrian school built upon this spirit began with Plato and Aristotle.

Greek science gradually merged from metaphysics to semi-rationalism. Not until experimental and observational techniques were introduced could scientific concepts be free from pure philosophical speculation·and form a solid and empirical basis for further progress. The Alexandrian school brought about a complete reversal of scientific procedure and made conditions favorable to scientific inquiry, asking not why nature operates, but how.

In the history of philosophy Plato (427–347 B.C.) was probably the greatest of Greek philosophers. What he inherited from the past, particularly from the Pythagorean school in the science of astronomy and mathematics, he advanced philosophically; that is, he gave an interpretation new to his age and, interestingly, still acceptable in the present. In his book, *Isaac Newton, A Biography*, Louis T. More says on page 258, "Although Plato added nothing to experimental science, yet his clearly expressed doctrine, that the determination of things by mathematical formulae is linked at the same time to their reality and their perceptibility, was an undying service to science."

Aristotle was one of the founders of the inductive method, and was the first to conceive the idea of organized research. He contributed considerably to the organization of science by his systematic survey and classification of the knowledge of his time. Aristotle may be called the founder of logic. His systematization of logic in the *Organon* was so masterful that it still dominates much of the teaching of today. He prepared the systematization of geometry by his investigations of its more fundamental and philosophical aspects, in particular by his introduction of new or better definitions and his discussion of the concepts of continuity and infinity. He completed the system of homocentric spheres of Eudoxus and Callippus, using a total of 55 spheres to account for all the celestial motions. His is the oldest attempt to estimate the size of the earth. Aristotle is the author of eight books on physics, four on the heavens, and four on meteorology.

The birth and transition of experimental procedure in scientific investigation can be traced from the academies of Plato and Aristotle to Archimedes of the Alexandrian school in clear, successive phases which became the basis of our modern science. Observation and experiment in mathematics combined gave Greek science a rationalistic and intellectual stimulation which ultimately gave to the world the finest products of Greek scientific genius. The link between Plato, Aristotle, and Archimedes was, of course, Euclid (323–285 B.C.), who became the first scholar of the Alexandrian school. His principal work was called *Elements*, which was in part a compilation of the works of earlier scholars, such as Pythagoras and Hippocrates. Its immense influence on the subsequent history of mathematics and the development of mechanics is well known. Some of the early editions of Euclid's works are represented in the Collection. They include:

The elements of geometrie of the most auncient philosopher Euclide of Megara. Faithfully (now first) translated into the Englishe toung, by H. Billingsley . . . With a very fruitfull praeface made by M. I. Dee . . . London, 1570.

Elementorum libri XV. Unà cum scholijs antiquis, à Federico Commandino Urbinate nuper in latinum conuersi, commentarijsque quibusdam illustrati. Pisauri, 1572.

Compendium Euclidis curioso: or, Geometrical operations . . . propositions of Evclid's first five books are performed. Tr. out of Dutch into English, by Joseph Moxon . . . London, 1677.

Euclidis data. Opus ad veterum geometriae autorum Archimedis, Apollonij, Pappi, Eutocij, caeterorúmque non modo lectionem, sed ad geometricae . . . Adiectus est ex eadem bibliotheca Marini philosophi commentarius graecè & latinè . . . Parisiorum, 1625.

Euclidis Elementorum libri XV, breviter demonstrati, operâ Is. Barrow . . . Cantabrigiae, 1655. Another edition, London, 1659. Also London, 1678.

The origins of the sciences of mechanics and hydrostatics are to be sought in the work of Archimedes and were placed on a sound footing when observation was allied to the deductive method. Archimedes investigated a large number of problems such as relative densities of bodies, the center of gravity of plane figures, principles of the lever, and so forth. He also investigated a number of astronomical and optical problems. Much of the foundation upon which Newton built his great success was taken from Archimedes' writings. It appears that the concept of gravity was first used by Archimedes, for heretofore the early Greeks had had no notion of the force of gravitation, but postulated the concept that a body is held in space due to the fact that it was in equilibrium, or just in the center of space. Archimedes is represented in the Collection by nine volumes including:

Archimedis opera qvae extant. Novis demonstrationibvs commentariisqve illvstrata. Per Davidem Rivaltvm a Flvrantia . . . Parisiis, 1615.

3

Archimedis opera: Apollonii Pergaei Conicorum, libri IIII. Theodosii Sphaerica: methodo nova illustrata, & succincte demonstrata. Per Is. Barrow . . . Londini, 1675.

Monumenta omnia mathematica, quae extant, quorumque catalogorum inuersa pagina demonstrat, ex traditione . . . Francisci Maurolici . . . Panormi, 1685.

Zwey Bücher über Kugel und Cylinder ebendesselben Kreismessung. Uebersezt, mit Anmerkungen und einem Anhang von Säzen über Kugel, Kugelstüke, und durch Umdrehung ebener regulärer Figuren entstehende Körper aus Lucas Valerius, Tacquet und Torricelli begleitet von Karl Friderich Hauber. Tübingen, 1798.

The works of Archimedes, edited in modern notation with introductory chapters, by T. L. Heath. Cambridge, England, 1897.

Archimedes door Dr. E. J. Dijksterhuis. Groningen, P. Noordhoff, 1938–

Apollonius of Perga studied under the successors of Euclid at the Alexandrian school. His chief work was the study of conic sections. Apollonius was also a student of optics and astronomy. He is represented in the Collection by:

Apollonii Pergaei Conicorum libri octo, et Sereni Antissensis De sectione cylindri & coni libri due. Oxoniae, 1710.

Apollonii Pergaei Inclinationum libri duo. Restituebat Samuel Horsley, R.S.S. Oxonii, 1770.

Eratosthenes (c. 276–c. 196 B.C.), Alexandrian astronomer, geometer, geographer, grammarian, and philosopher, has been called "the founder of astronomical geography and of scientific chronology." He measured the obliquity of the ecliptic, and introduced a method of computing the earth's magnitude. Only fragments of his *Geographica* are extant.

Aristarchus (310–230 B.C.) was known as the Copernicus of antiquity and a natural philosopher of originality. He flourished about 280 B.C. and was one of the few men that possessed a profound knowledge of the mathematical sciences of his period. His only extant work, a work which proved his geometrical powers, was concerned with the size and distance of the sun and moon. There is no doubt that Aristarchus advanced the heliocentric hypothesis. This was acknowledged by Archimedes. In 1543–though this is not generally known—Copernicus admitted his hypothesis of the motion of the earth was based upon the work of Aristarchus. Probably no scholar of the early Greek period advanced science to such a degree. He clearly established for all times the famous dictum of "saving the phenomena" as well as placing science upon a rational basis. The following edition of his only work is in the Collection:

Aristarchi De magnitvdinibvs, et distantiis solis, et lvnae, liber; cvm

Pappi Alexandrıni explicationibus quibusdam. A'Federico Commandıno Vrbinate in latınum conuersus, ac commentarıjs illustratus. Cum priuilegio pont. max. in annos x. Pisavri, MDLXXII.

In the second century A.D., the Alexandrian school was beginning to lose its supremacy ın Greek learnıng. One of the last of the important Greek geometricians was Hero (c. 150), a mathematician, physicist, and inventor, He found the algebraic solution of equations of the first and second degree and worked out many formulae for the measurement of areas and volumes. In optics, he pointed out that the line of reflected light ıs the shortest path. The Collection contains a copy of one of hıs books:

Heronis Alexandrıni spiritalıvm liber. A Federico Commandino vrbinate, ex graeco, nvper in latinvm conversvs . . . Urbini, 1575.

Greek astronomy found its last cultivator and expounder in Claudius Ptolemæus who flourished about 140 A.D. His principal work in astronomy was the *Syntaxis,* commonly known as the *Almagest,* which term is taken from the Arabic translation. In his work Ptolemæus undertook to present for the first time the whole history of astronomical science. His theory of the solar system, namely the arrangement of the planets, is known as the geocentric, due to the fact that the earth was the center of his system and that the sun and planets revolved about it. It remained a curious fact that Ptolemæus based his theory on the observations of Hipparchus' (c. 160–125 B.C.) *Catalogue of Stars and Planets,* which were supposed to be the most accurate of the time, but his own work, the *Almagest,* remained the authoritative work for over 1,500 years and was not superseded until Copernicus revised the system of planetary motion in 1543 and it became known as the heliocentric system. Two early editions of Ptolemaeus' works are in the Collection:

Almagestũ Cl. Ptolemei Pheludıensis Alexandrıni astronomor principis: Opus ingens ac nobıle omnes celorũ motus continens. Felicibus astris eat in lucex: ductu Petri Liechtenstein Coloniesis Germani. Anno virginei partus 1515.

Beobachtung und Beschreibung der Gestirne und der Bewegung der himmlischen Sphäre; mit Erläuterungen, Vergleıchungen der neuern Beobachtungen und einem stereographıschen Entwurf der beyden Halbkugeln des gestırnten Himmels für die Zeit des Ptolemäus, von J. E. Bode. Berlin, 1795.

With the end of the Ptolemaic period and the fall of the Alexandrian school, Greek and Roman science merged. The schools of Plato and Aristotle were closed in 529 by the Emperor Justinian. The Collection contains no editions of the writings of the scientific thinkers of the Roman

5

period, such as men like Pliny (23–79) and Boethius (480–524), who kept alive the study of pure science and mathematics, and especially medicine.

While European knowledge was at its lowest ebb, a considerable amount of scientific work of mixed Greek, Roman, and Jewish origin was conducted in the Byzantine imperial court at Constantinople. Two other early centers of learning were the Persian and Arabian schools at Babylonia and Baghdad, where the Caliphs encouraged translations of the Greek authors. In southern Spain the invading Moors brought with them the forgotten stores of Greek science which were translated from the Arabic and Greek into Latin. Mathematics and physics were also studied but very little original work can be traced to the Mohammedan scholars, although the Collection does contain an early edition of the Optics of Alhazen (965–1039):

> *Opticae thesavrvs. Alhazeni Arabis libri septem, nuncprimùm editi. Eivsdem liber De crepvscvlis & nubium ascensionibus. Item Vitellonis Thvringopoloni libri x. Omnes instaurati, figuris illustrati & aucti, adiectis etiam in Alhazenum commentarijs,* à Federico Risnero. Basileae, 1572.

A touch of Hindu influence was introduced about 980 when the Arabian scholars and mathematicians studied and in part translated the writings of Brahmagupta's (c. 598–c. 660) arithmetic and algebra. This work is in the Collection, together with other Hindu mathematical works of the period·

> *Brahmegupta and Bháscara. Algebra, with Arithmetic and Mensuration, from the Sanscrit.* Translated by Henry Thomas Colebrooke, Esq. London, 1817.

> Bhaskaracharya. *Siddhanta s'iromani (a treatise on astronomy)* . . . ed. by Pandit Bapu Deva Sastri, C.I.E. (Kaski Sanskrit series). Banaras, 1950.

> *Bakhshali manuscript: a study in mediaeval mathematics.* Edited by George R. Kaye. Calcutta, 1927.

> *Jyautishasiddhantasangraha (a collection of ancient Hindu astronomical works)* . . . edited by Pandit V. P. Dvivedi. (Banaras Sanskrit series. Complete in 2 fasc., nos. 152 & 154).

The Renaissance Scholars

A new spirit arose in Europe in the thirteenth century. We cannot fail to detect at this time the existence, even at places as far apart as Oxford and Bologna, of a widespread desire for knowledge and a zeal for learning such as had not been known for centuries. Arabic mathematical science was introduced into Europe by Leonardo Pisano. Fresh and notable philos-

6

ophers and humanists including Albertus Magnus, Thomas Aquinas, and, most noteworthy of all for the history of science, Roger Bacon, were among the important scholars of the early Renaissance.

Roger Bacon was a man thoroughly acquainted with the astronomical writings of both Greeks and Arabs. At Oxford he was under the influence of Robert Grosse-Teste, afterwards Bishop of Lincoln, who had devoted some attention to astronomy and was a follower of Ptolemæus. It was not until Bacon went to Paris around 1235 that he began to study scientific problems seriously. On the question of Aristotle's *Physics*, Bacon showed more knowledge, especially of the system of Eudoxus, than any of his associates. Subsequent writings of Bacon show his persevering study of cosmology and astronomy; but he continued all his life to hesitate between the two systems of the world.

Roger Bacon (1214–1294) was educated at Oxford and Paris and joined the Franciscan Order. Much has been written about this most interesting friar, but suffice it to say here that his works linked the Islamic learning to that of the Renaissance. Bacon advanced the doctrine of experimentalism and rationalism, that is, that the study of mathematics was fundamental to experiment. (The University Library has on its shelves the *Opus Magnus* of Roger Bacon, as well as translations, various editions, commentaries, and criticisms.)

By the beginning of the thirteenth century, the works of Aristotle and of other Greek scientists were gradually making their way into the Western world, through translations direct from the Greek and Latin versions of Arabic translations. Aristotle was accepted as the final authority on metaphysics, moral philosophy, and natural science.

It was in Italy that the Latin world first came into contact with the half-forgotten treasures of Greek wisdom. The Englishman Ádelard of Bath (c. 1116–c. 1142) translated Euclid into Latin during the first half of the eleventh century in Italy. The algebra and the arithmetic which the Arabs had borrowed from the Hindus were introduced into Italy in the first years of the following century by the Pisan merchant, Leonardo Fibonacci (c. 1170–c. 1240). It was to this Arabo-Greek influence that Bologna owed its very important School of Medicine and Mathematics—two subjects more closely connected then than now through their common relationship to astrology. The new humanism and astronomy were being argued by Nicholas of Cusa (1401–1464) who stated that the universe was infinite in extent and could have no center. In mathematics he followed Euclid and Archimedes. Georg von Peurbach (1423–1461), a brilliant student of Cusa in Rome, later became a professor of astronomy and mathematics at the University of Vienna. He was called the founder of observational and mathematical astronomy. The Collection contains the following edition of Peurbach's work:

🐚 *Theoricae novae planetarum Georgii Purbachii Germani ab Erasmo Reinholdo Salueldensi pluribus figuris auctae, & illustratae scholiis, quibus studiosi praeparentur, ac inuitentur ad lectionem ipsius Ptolemaei.* Wittenberg, 1542.

Peurbach's most eminent pupil and successor was John Müller (1436–1476) of Königsberg, who combined science with humanism. He translated into Latin the works of Ptolemaeus and other Greek writers. Leonardo da Vinci is not represented in the Collection but should be considered a connecting link between the Greek and Renaissance schools, in particular between Archimedes and Roger Bacon.

The genius of Hipparchus and Ptolemaeus had brought astronomy to its culmination. Higher it could not rise until three conditions were fulfilled—first, better astronomical instruments and more accurate observations extended over longer periods; second, more improved mathematical computations, particularly for reduction and interpretation of these observations; and third, a substantial progress toward clearer thinking regarding the fundamental laws and facts pertaining to the motion of the planets. These conditions were met during the sixteenth and seventeenth centuries and the new astronomy exemplified by the work of such giants as Copernicus, Kepler, Galileo, Descartes, and Gassendi went forth with magnificent progress.

Nicolaus Copernicus (1473–1543), a Polish theologian and astronomer, was the founder of modern astronomy. He became a canon at Frauenburg, near Königsberg, Germany, in 1497. From 1512 until his death thirty years later, he rendered various public services, practiced medicine, and devoted much time to astronomical studies. In his study of the classical writers he came upon a statement that certain Pythagorean philosophers and the Alexandrian astronomer Aristarchus explained the phenomena of the daily and yearly motions of the heavenly bodies by supposing the earth itself to rotate on its axis and to have an orbital motion. His confirmation of this theory was published in his famous thesis *De Orbium Celestium Revolutionibus* in 1543, which established the Copernican system of astronomy. Copernicus is represented in the Collection by the following works:

🐚 *Nicolaus Coppernicus aus Thorn Über die Kreisbewegungen der Weltkörper.* Übersetzt und mit Anmerkungen von Dr. C. L. Menzzer. Durchgesehen und mit einem Vorwort von Dr. Moritz Cantor. Thorn, 1879.

🐚 *Die vierte Säcularfeier der Geburt von Nicolaus Copernicus.* Thorn 18. und 19. Februar 1873 . . . Berlin, 1874.

Three Copernican treatises: the Commentariolus of Copernicus, the Letter against Werner, the Narratio prima of Rheticus; . . . Translated with introduction and notes by Edward Rosen. New York, 1939.

Johann Kepler (1571–1630) was one of the most distinguished astronomers of the Renaissance. Astronomy, mathematics, and astrology were of particular concern to him, and this interest led to his zealous research into the size and motion of the heavenly bodies. He sought reality in the mathematical aspects of the planetary order. Kepler had succeeded Tycho Brahe (1546–1601) as the Imperial Mathematician at Prague in 1602 and inherited a great collection left by Brahe at his death. Among all the planetary observations of Brahe, those of Mars presented irregularities most difficult to explain. Since these were originally assigned to Kepler, they engrossed his attention for many years and in the end led to his finest discoveries. His scientific imagination led him to the great discovery that the planet traverses its orbit in such a manner that a line joining it to the sun would describe sectors of equal area in equal times, the planet thus moving fastest when nearest the sun. From this study he discovered the three laws of planetary motions, the first two being: (1) the planet describes an ellipse, the sun being in one focus, and (2) the straight line joining the planet to the sun sweeps out equal areas in equal intervals of time. Results were published in 1609 as part of the extended *Commentaries on the Motions of Mars.* The third law stating that the square of the times of revolution of any two planets (including the earth) about the sun are proportional to the cubes of their mean distances from the sun was discovered in 1619 and was published in his book *Harmony of the World.* These three geometrical laws became the basis of Newton's three dynamical laws. The following editions of Kepler's works are among those included in the Collection:

Opera omnia; ed. Ch. Frisch. Frankofurti am. M., Heyder & Zimmer, 1858–1871.

Epitome astronomiae Copernicanae usitata forma quaestionum & responsionum conscripta, inq; VII . . . Lentijs, 1618.

Dioptrice: seu Demonstratio eorum quae visui & visilibus propter conspicilla non ita pridem inventa accidunt . . . Londini, 1653.

Bibliographia Kepleriana. Ein Führer Durch Das Gedruckte Schrifttum von Johannes Kepler . . . Herausgegeben von Max Caspar. München, 1936.

Galileo (1564–1642), the Italian physicist and astronomer, was born in Pisa. He studied at the University of Pisa and taught mathematics there, later serving at Padua and Florence. In 1583, while watching a lamp swinging in the cathedral at Pisa, he discovered that oscillations of the lamps could be used to time his pulse. From this he deduced the isochronic nature of the swing of the pendulum which he later demonstrated might be used to measure time. In 1586 he invented the hydrostatic balance, an instrument for determining the specific gravities of substances by comparing their weights in and out of water. He also developed an experiment to determine the speed of light, but the timing mechanisms then in use were too inaccurate to measure the extremely small time intervals involved, and the experiment came to nothing. According to a famous story, he dropped bodies of various weights from the Leaning Tower of Pisa and thus showed that all bodies would fall with equal velocities in a vacuum. He continued his experiments with falling bodies with the use of the inclined plane, from which experiments he developed theories relative to motion that were later to be demonstrated as laws by Isaac Newton. He showed also that the parabola of a projectile's flight was made up of a horizontal and a vertical component, and that the latter was ruled by the same forces that governed falling bodies. He invented the first thermometer in 1597, and the first telescope in 1609. With this instrument, magnifying to about 30 diameters, Galileo discovered (1610) that Jupiter had satellites (he saw four of them), that Saturn was surrounded by rings, that the moon's surface was mountainous and not smooth, that Venus went through phases like the moon's (due to its position between Earth and Sun). He noted (1610) the existence of sunspots and developed thence the idea that the sun rotated on its axis; and he stated that, given a better telescope, an observer might resolve the Milky Way into individual stars. His publication of *Letters on the Solar Spots* (1613) embodied his acceptance of the Copernican system of the universe, which made of the earth a mere planet circling about the sun instead of the fixed center of the universe (which it was according to the Ptolemaic theory). He was summoned to Rome where, in 1616, his doctrines, which he had attempted to justify by Biblical quotation, were condemned as heretical by the Pope. An essay on comets, *Saggiatore,* which he published in 1623, was well received, however, despite several oblique defenses of the Copernican system. But the publication of *Dialogo dei due massimi sistemi del mondo (Dialogue on the Two Chief Systems of the Universe)* in 1632 caused a storm. It was acclaimed all over Europe, but its advocacy of Copernicanism, despite the papal injunction of 1616, brought down the wrath of the Church on his head. The book was banned by Rome and Galileo was called (1633) before the Inquisition. There, under the threat of torture, he was forced to abjure his belief in the Copernican theory; the familiar legend states that as he arose after his recantation he murmured: "Eppur si muove" (And yet it does move). As a result of his quarrel with the Church, he was removed from his academic posts and retired to his home at Arcetri. There, despite almost total blindness, he discovered (1637) the moon's libration (presentation of more than half its surface to the view of observers on earth). Galileo's *Dialoghi delle nuove scienzi* (1638) summed up his experiments and theories on mechanics. Galileo established the method of modern science, a deductive-inductive method that verifies theory by practical experiment and surrenders the rationalized, universal "proofs" of scholasticism for the amassing of data, later to be systematized by theory, in limited fields. The following titles are in the Collection:

    Dialogo di Galileo Galilei Linceo matematico sopraordinario dello stvdio di Pisa. E filosofo, e matematico primario del serenissimo gr. dvca di Toscana . . . Fiorenza, 1632. This edition was suppressed by the Inquisition in 1633.

    Systema cosmicum: in quo dialogis IV de duobus maximis mundi systematibus, ptolemaico & copernicano, rationibus utrinque propositis indefinitè disseritur . . . Lugduni, 1641.

    Opere. Milano, Società tipografica de'classici italiani, 1808–11. 13 v. Milano.

René Descartes (1596–1650), the French philosopher and mathematician, graduated at the age of 17 from the Jesuit college of La Flèche and later studied at the University of Poitiers, saw some brief military service, lived for a time at Paris, and spent several years in travel, visiting Germany, Italy, Holland, and Poland, studying and seeking knowledge. In 1629 he took up residence in Holland, where he lived a retired life, busily engaged, however, in elaborating and defending his philosophy and formulating his mathematical system. In 1649, upon the invitation of Queen Christina of Sweden, he went to Stockholm, only to die there of pneumonia five months later. Descartes' importance as a modern philosopher was established in 1637 when his brief treatise *Discours de la méthode,* which set forth his theories, was published.

Descartes rejected scholasticism and based his speculations upon pure reason, his point of basic approach being derived from his famous axiom, Cogito, ergo sum (I think, therefore I am). Willing to take nothing for granted (the point of the axiom cited above is, of course, that it enabled Descartes safely to assume his own existence), he proceeds to proof of the existence of God, and from that to a demonstration of the reality of the material world. Between the material world and the mind or soul he posits a complete gulf, which can be bridged only by the direct intervention of God. Writing at a time when speculation could take its stand upon pure reason (still within the framework of Roman Catholic theology), his system inevitably diminished in authority with the rise, beginning a century or so after his death, of the natural sciences as they have since come to be understood. Descartes is represented in the Collection with the following editions:

Renati Des-Cartes Principia philosophiae. Amstelodami, apud Ludovicum Elzevirium, 1644.

Principia philosophiae. Amstelodami, Apud J. Jansonium juniorem, 1656. . . . With this is bound his *Specimina philosophiae: seu Dissertatio de methodo rectè regendae rationis . . .* Amstelodami, 1656.

Specimina philosophiae; seu Dissertatio de methodo rectè regendae rationis, & veritatis in scientiis investigandae . . . Amstelodami, 1656.

Opera philosophica. Editio quarta, nunc demum hac editione diligenter recognita, & mendis expurgata. 3 v. in 1. Amstelodami, 1664.

Epistolae, partim ab auctore latino sermone conscriptae, partim ex gallico translatae. In quibus omnis generis quaestiones philosophicae tractantur, & explicantur plurimae difficultates quae in reliquis ejus operibus occurrunt. 2 v. in 1. Amstelodami, 1668. Another edition, Amstelodami, 1682.

Geometria, unà cum notis Florimondi de Beaune . . . & commentariis illustrata, opera atque studio Francisci à Schooten . . . Francofurti, 1695.

Pierre Gassendi (1592–1655), a French philosopher, physicist, and astronomer, studied theology at Digne, became professor of theology there in 1613, and later taught philosophy at Aix. In 1645 he became professor of mathematics at the Collège Royal at Paris. He sought to link the philosophy of Epicurus with Christian theology and modern science. Among his works are the *Disquisitiones anticartesianae* and the *De vita, moribus, et placitis Epicuri* (1647). Editions of his works in the Collection are:

Institutio astronomica, juxta hypotheses tam veterum quàm recentiorum. Cui accesserunt Galilei Galilei Nuntius sidereus, et Johannis Kepleri Dioptrice. Secunda editio priori correctior. Londini, 1653.

Tychonis Brahei, equitis dani., astronomorum coryphaei, vita. Authore Petro Gassendo . . . Accessit Nicolai Copernici, Georgii Peurbachii, & Joannis Regiomontani, astronomorum celebrium vita. Hagae, 1655.

Institutio astronomica juxta hypotheses tam veterum quàm Copernici & Tychonis: dicta Parisiis a Petro Gassendo . . . Accedunt ejusdem varij tractatus astronomici . . . Amstelaedami, 1680.

The Forerunners of Newton

The story of scientific research in seventeenth century England is the story of the Royal Society of London. The Royal Society began as a series of informal meetings at Gresham College in London of men more or less learned, but all deeply interested in experimental knowledge. Included in this group of scientists were John Wallis, a mathematician, and Dr. John Wilkins, a very ingenious man who had a mechanical mind. Wilkins later became a famous mathematician and astronomer. Samuel Foster, professor of astronomy at Gresham College, worked primarily on astronomical instruments. Several members of the Royal College of Physicians were in the group, including Dr. Jonathan Goddard, Cromwell's physician and a professor of medicine at Gresham College, where he had a laboratory for "Chymistrie."

Meeting first in London at Gresham College or in their private apartments, they later moved to Oxford where they were joined by Christopher Wren, Seth Ward, and Laurence Rooke. In 1662 the Society received a charter from King Charles II and became the Royal Society of London. From this date on, the scientific atmosphere in London and on the Continent became very much alive and active. The *Philosophical Transactions* published by the Society immediately became the most versatile and sought-after scientific journal. The first forty volumes contain the writings of Newton on light, his experiments and results, and also the writings of Edmund Halley, Robert Hooke, and many of the other contemporary scholars. The first ninety volumes, 1665–1800, are shelved in the Collection.

France and Italy also established Academies of Science during this period and each had its publication. The scientific journal of the Germans, the *Acta Eruditorum,* which was published monthly at Leipzig beginning in 1682, was quite similar to *Philosophical Transactions.* It contains the writings of the important German scholars, including Leibniz. The Collection contains the first forty-seven volumes, 1683–1731.

Two of the men closest to Newton in his research and philosophical work were John Locke and Robert Boyle. Those who were closest to Newton in his scientific work were Isaac Barrow, Edmund Halley, David Gregory, and Colin Maclaurin. Following are brief sketches of each of those men, all of whom are represented in the Collection.

John Locke (1632–1704), a great English philosopher as well as a close friend of Isaac Newton, was born in Somersetshire, England. Just when he became acquainted with Isaac Newton is not known but they had much in common regarding religion. The Newton Collection contains the London, 1720, edition of *A Collection of Several Pieces of Mr. John Locke, Never before printed, or not extant in his Works.*

Robert Boyle (1627–1691), another of Newton's great friends, was born at Lismore Castle, Ireland. He regarded the acquisition of knowledge as an end in itself and thereby gained a wider view of the aims of scientific inquiry than was shown by the majority of his predecessors. He protested against the current practice of considering chemistry simply as an aid to the preparation of medicines or to the improvement of metals. Our present-day chemical concepts of element, compound, and decomposition stem from Boyle, and it was he who first stated that it is necessary to investigate the elementary constituents into which the substances found in nature can be decomposed, thereby introducing our present concept of the elements. Boyle's famous discovery which states that the pressure of a gas is proportional to the number of molecules present in a given space and to their temperature, that is, the average value of their energy of motion, is known as Boyle's Law. This Collection is fortunate to have six volumes of Boyle's works, three of which seem to have had the greatest influence on Newton's thinking, and are listed here:

Experiments and considerations touching colours . . . London, 1664.

The origine of formes and qualities, (according to the corpuscular philosophy) illustrated by considerations and experiments . . . Oxford, 1667.

Essays of the strange subtilty, determinate nature, great efficacy of effluviums. To which are annext New experiments to make fire and flame ponderable: together with A discovery of the perviousness of glass. London, 1673.

The Collection is also fortunate to have a copy of what is probably the best-known bibliography of Robert Boyle, which was prepared by the late Dr. J. F. Fulton of Yale University, who is recognized as the foremost Boyle scholar of recent times.

Undoubtedly two of the most important individuals in the life and work of Isaac Newton were Dr. Isaac Barrow and Dr. Edmund Halley. They were known as the scientific godfathers of young Newton. Isaac Barrow (1630–1677) was an English theologian, a classical scholar, and a mathematician. He was educated at Cambridge and was appointed professor of geometry at Gresham College. In 1663 he became the first Lucasian professor of mathematics at Cambridge, a post from which he resigned in 1669 in favor of Newton, and in 1672 was appointed master of Trinity College. Among his works in the Collection is the *Lectiones Opticae et Geometricae* (1669, 1670–74).

Edmund Halley (1656–1742) studied at St. Paul's School and Queen's College, Oxford, but left the University in 1676 without taking a degree. His astronomical studies were begun in his boyhood (his first communication to the Royal Society of London was sent before he was 20), and in 1676 he sailed for St. Helena to observe the positions of the fixed stars in the Southern Hemisphere in order to make astronomical calculations more accurate. Others were then at work on the Northern Hemisphere. On November 7, 1677, at St. Helena, he made "the first complete observation of a transit of Mercury" and in 1678 was elected a Fellow of the Royal Society where he became successively assistant secretary, secretary of the Society, and editor (1685–1693) of the *Philosophical Transactions*. He was appointed Savilian professor of geometry at Oxford in 1703 and was appointed successor to Flamsteed as Astronomer Royal in 1721. From November, 1698, to September, 1700, he explored the South Atlantic in the *Paramour Pink* (returning once to England) for the purpose of studying the variation of the compass and discovering southern lands. In 1701, in the same vessel, he surveyed the tides and coasts of the English Channel. He is best known for his studies of comets. He inferred from his computations that the comets of 1531, 1607, and 1682 were in reality the same body, and predicted its return in 1758, a prediction which was verified by its appearance on Christmas day of that year. This comet has since been known by his name. The following works of Halley's are in the Collection:

Astronomical tables with precepts, both in English and Latin, for computing places of the sun, moon, planets, and comets. London, 1752.

Miscellaneous curiosa. Containing a collection of some of the principal phænomena in nature, accounted for by the greatest philosophers of this age: being the most valuable discourses, read and delivered to the Royal Society, for the advancement of physical and mathematical knowledge . . . London, 1723–27.

Correspondence and papers of Edmond Halley, preceded by an unpublished memoir of his life by one of his contemporaries and the 'Eloge' by D'Ortous de Mairan; arranged and edited by Eugene Fairfield MacPike . . . Oxford, 1932.

David Gregory (1661–1708), a Scottish astronomer, became professor of mathematics at Edinburgh in 1683 and was "the first professor who publicly lectured on the Newtonian philosophy." In 1691 he was appointed Savilian professor of astronomy at Oxford and became a fellow of the Royal Society in 1692. The 1702 edition of his work, the *Astronomiae physicae et geometricae elementa,* is in the Collection. He also edited the works of Euclid (1703) and left several treatises in manuscript.

Colin Maclaurin (1698–1746), a mathematician and physicist, did important work in calculus, especially on maxima and minima, and indicated the solution of the problem of tides, the shape of the earth, and other phenomena connected with the revolution of a fluid body. He wrote *Geometria Organica, sive Descriptio Linearum Curvarium Universalis* (1720), *A Treatise of Fluxions* (1742), *A Treatise of Algebra, with an Appendix De Linearum Geometricarum Proprietatibus Generalibus* (1748), and *An Account of Sir Isaac Newton's Philosophy* (1748), all of which are in the Collection.

We consider the immortal *Principia* to be the keystone of the Stanford Newton Collection. Therefore, although the Collection contains one hundred and six editions of other Newton works, including the *Opticks*, *Arithmetica Universalis*, and the *Chronologie*, we will only make comments on the history of the *Principia* in this essay.

The generic development of the great work by Isaac Newton, the *Principia*—properly known as *Philosophiae Naturalis Principia Mathematica*—may be said to have its origin in antiquity, certainly as far back as the Alexandrian epoch. It is to Archimedes particularly, however, that credit can be given for being the scientific forefather of Isaac Newton. He it was who paved the way for the *Principia* and modern scientific synthesis. Archimedes studied the geometry of measurements dealing with the quadrature of curvilinear plane figures and with the quadrature and cubature of curved surfaces, investigations which "gave birth to the calculus of the infinite conceived and brought to perfection successively by Kepler, Cavalieri, Fermat, Leibniz, and Newton." Archimedes also experimented on fluids and solids, and by geometric induction established the concept of gravity. In the earlier Greek period this concept was postulated as a force without definite mathematical or physical properties.

The vicissitudes of the concept of gravity in the scientific revolution that came about during the period of transition from the science of antiquity and the medieval period to the Newtonian epoch are, in essence, the basis of the history of the physical sciences. Beginning with the modern age, however, a few of the early leaders in scientific thought might be mentioned. The most important of these was Copernicus who conceived the central force to be a "certain affinity or a natural tendency of matter." Various other physical concepts of the nature of the force of attraction and inertia were developed by William Gilbert (1544–1603). He assumed that motion and attraction were due to magnetic-electrical phenomena. Stevin (1548–1620) was the first to investigate the mechanics of the inclined plane, and developed the principle of symmetry that equilibrium subsists. Kepler states that "no point, no center is heavy, but everything of the same nature as a body will tend to it, nor does the center acquire weight by drawing other things to it any more than a magnet gets heavier while drawing iron." With Galileo, it seems that terrestrial gravity and universal gravitation have apparently different connotations. Galileo's laws of falling bodies were understood with difficulty by scholars of the period due to the fact that Descartes' vortex theory was widely accepted. The doctrine of gravity of Descartes supposed the revolution of fine invisible particles in a vortex whirling in planes perpendicular to the earth's axis. Gassendi considered the gravity of a body as an external force depending on the presence and properties of other bodies. The fundamental physical assumption of Huygens rested on the theory of a force having a centrifugal tendency, which caused the subtle matter revolving around the earth to force the large particles of earthly bodies toward the center.

Nevertheless it was reserved for Isaac Newton to give a complete, rational, and definite mathematical expression to the physical force acting upon material bodies in space. This was accomplished by Newton's investigation of the moon's motion and deviation of the centrifugal force, and also by his study of Kepler's second law of motion and the nature of the force acting to cause a planet to revolve about the sun in an ellipse. From his investigations in both these fields, Newton derived his famous inverse square law, namely, $F = k(m_1 m_2)/r^2$, where m equals mass and r the radius. This formula gave a degree of finality to what had hitherto been mere speculation regarding the laws governing the nature of any system of the known universe and was the first great scientific synthesis.

The ground work for Newton's scientific achievements was laid during his student days at Trinity College, Cambridge—his meditations and discoveries here were to be most profitable indeed for the future of science. Here too he found the tutor cognizant of his ability, Isaac Barrow, the most distinguished geometer of his period. Under this good man, Newton was introduced to the classical scholars of the Alexandrian school, Apollonius and Archimedes. (It appears in fact that Newton followed Archimedes' classical methodology almost entirely in the preparation of the *Principia*.) He made such great progress in his mathematical studies that Barrow later resigned his tutorship in favor of his student.

During the plague years, 1665–1666, Newton, having just graduated and having been appointed Junior Fellow of the College, retired to his mother's home in Woolsthrope near Grantham, fifty miles north of Cambridge. With a mind full of speculative ideas on the current problems in astronomy, mathematics, and optics, Newton was prepared to give thought to those that most interested him. In the two years of enforced retirement he discovered the law of gravitation, the concept of fluxions, and the color of light. Upon his return to the College he continued his studies, particularly in gravitation and the spectrum of light. In addition, he made experiments in alchemy, undoubtedly seeking the law of affinity, and later on became an excellent scholar in theology and chronology. As yet he had made no public announcement of his great discoveries except to his tutor, Dr. Barrow.

As a Fellow of Trinity College, Newton gave lectures on optics and astronomy which were primarily on the motion of bodies in space. These lectures, entitled "De Motu Corporum" attracted few students, often none at all. "De Motu Corporum" was the forerunner of the *Principia.*

Halley, from consideration of the third law of Kepler, had come to the conclusion that the centripetal force of attraction was inversely proportional to the square of the distance. But, not being able to prove it, he went up to Cambridge where he had heard that a young man at the university had the answer. Halley, upon meeting Newton, asked the question, "What would be the curve described by the planets on the supposition that gravity diminished as the square of the distance?" Newton immediately answered, "An ellipse." Halley was so struck with joy and amazement, that he asked Newton how he knew it. Newton replied, "I have calculated it." Thereupon, Halley returned to London to give the answer to his colleagues. From then on, under Halley's enthusiastic encouragement, Newton proceeded to work further on the subject. After his discovery of the inverse square law, Newton undertook to examine all the physical phenomena in the solar system. Then followed seventeen months of intense work, with Newton at times not taking his meals or sleep. During this time he completed the manuscript of his immortal work. Halley presented the manuscript to the Royal Society, but in view of the fact that the Society did not have sufficient funds to publish it, Halley again came to the rescue and financed this work through the press. In 1687 the *Principia* was published and given to a world unprepared to understand its great importance. Newton himself realized that the layman would need preparation before undertaking the study of the *Principia* and the modern reader also would do well to follow Newton's advice to his own contemporaries. (It is not intended that the particular books so recommended by Newton be studied, but of course more modern texts of similar character.)

> Next after Euclid's Elements the Elements of y Conic Sections are to be understood. And for this end you may read either the first part of y Elementa Curvarum of John De Witt, or De la Hire's late treatise of y conick sections, or D Barrow's Epitome of Apollonius.
>
> For Algebra read first Bartholin's introduction, and then peruse such Problems as you will find scattered up and down in y Commentaries on Cartes's Geometry and other Alegraical [sic] writings of Franciss Schooten. I do not mean y you should read over all those Commentaries, but only y solutions of such Problems as you will here and there meet with. You may meet with De Witt's Elementa Curvarum and Bartholin's Introduction bound up together w Carte's Geometry and Schooten's Commentaries.
>
> For Astronomy read first y short account of y Copernician System in the end of Gassendus's Astronomy and then so much of Mercator's Astronomy as concerns y same system and the new discoveries made in the heavens by Telescopes in the Appendix.
>
> These are sufficient for understanding my book: but if you can procure

Hugenius's Horologium oscillatorium, the perusal of that will make you much more ready.

At y first perusal of my Book it's enough if you understand y Propositions w some of y Demonstrations w are easier than the rest. For when you understand y easier they will afterwards give you light into y harder. When you have read y first 60 pages, pass on to y 3 Book and when you see the design of that you may turn back to such Propositions as you shall have a desire to know, or peruse the whole in order if you think fit. (*An Essay on Newton's Principia,* by W. W. Rouse Ball.)

The *Principia* is composed of three books, a total of five hundred ten pages. Book I is given to the consideration of the motion of bodies in free space, either in known orbits or under the action of known forces or actions of mutual attraction. Here Newton generalizes the law of attraction into a statement that every particle of matter in the universe attracts every other particle with a force which varies directly as the product of their masses and inversely as the square of the distance between them. Book II treats of motion in a resisting medium of hydrostatics and hydrodynamics, with special reference to waves, tides, and acoustics. He concludes the Descartian theory of vortices is inconsistent with the laws of attraction and motion. Book III presents an explanation of the phenomena of the solar system, cometary orbits, perturbation, parallaxes of stars, and the famous General Scholium. Following the Preface there are 193 propositions and a great number of theorems, problems, lemmas and scholia, all based upon eight definitions and three axioms, laws of motion. These laws are deduced from Kepler's three laws of planetary motion and form the dynamic basis of the whole concept of the *Principia*. The *Principia* was prepared in the synthetical method made famous by the Greek geometers. This was done mainly because it could be best understood by his contemporaries, although it has been stated that Newton prepared many of his propositions by the analytical method invented by himself and perfected by Leibniz.

The *Principia* was published in Latin and about 250 copies were issued. It found immediate sale due to its novelty. In 1713 a second edition was issued under the very able young editor and scholar, Roger Cotes (1682–1716). He was an English mathematician, a graduate of Trinity College at Cambridge, and Plumian professor of astronomy at Trinity (1706). He was a friend of Newton's and aided him in preparing the second edition of the *Principia,* which appeared in 1713, for which he also wrote the preface. Their correspondence was published in 1850. Cotes published only one scientific treatise, *Logometria* (1713), during his life, but his papers were edited by Robert Smith and published in 1722 and 1738.

The second edition of the *Principia* was a thorough revision of the first, which was necessary because of the pressure brought to bear upon

Newton during the seventeen months in which he prepared the original. Cotes prepared a new preface of historical and philosophical interest and he also enlarged upon the famous General Scholium. This edition consisted of 750 copies. Both editions are new extremely rare. In 1726 the third edition, a revision of the second, was prepared by Henry Pemberton (1694–1771), a close friend of Newton's. This was the last edition prepared by Newton during his lifetime, and it is the only edition that contains the engraved portrait taken from the famous painting done by Vanderbank in 1725 when Newton was eighty-three. All subsequent editions of the *Principia,* including those issued in foreign languages, are in the Collection. Some of these are: the first English translation from the Latin, the third edition by A. Motte (London, 1729, 2 vols.), a new edition of the same (London, 1803, 3 vols.), French edition translated by the Marquise du Chastellet (Paris, 1759, 2 vols.), Italian edition translated by Nicola Fergola (Napoli, 1792–1793, 2 vols.), American edition, edited from A. Motte's first English edition, by N. W. Chittenden (New York, 1846), Glasgow edition, reprinted from the Latin third edition for Sir William Thomson and Hugh Blackburn (Glasgow, 1871), German edition translated by J. Ph. Wolfers (Berlin, 1872), Swedish edition translated by C. V. L. Charlier (Lund, 1927–1931, 3 vols.), Japanese edition translated by Kunion Oka (Tokyo, 1930), Dutch edition translated by H. J. E. Beth (Groningen, 1932, 2 vols.), Russian edition translated by Aleksei Krylov (Moscow, 1936), and the American edition, edited from the third edition by Florian Cajori (Berkeley, 1934, reissued 1946).

In a recent survey to determine the number and location of the first three original editions of the *Principia* still extant, it was found by Mr. H. P. Macomber, Curator of the Isaac Newton Collection in the Babson Institute Library, that a total of two hundred copies of the first edition, 1687, have been located. Also most interesting was the fact that sixty-four of these are now resting on the shelves of our university, college, and private libraries. In addition there are approximately forty-seven copies of the second edition, 1713, and forty copies of the third edition, 1726. Newton also had fifty copies of the third edition printed on heavy folio paper. Of these, twelve were bound in full Harleian red morocco leather, with beautiful gold decoration on the cover and back. These were for the various libraries of Oxford, Cambridge, the Royal Society, Oxford Observatory, the Academy of Science, Paris, and for a few special friends in France.

In addition to the above, the *Principia* is to be found in three collected editions, a large number of abridgements, reprints and sections for classroom purposes. As is to be expected in a work of this character, commentaries and philosophies of Newton's works abound even today.

Newton's laws became the first great synthesis of the known cosmos. His thought laid the foundation for further development in the fields of celestial mechanics, pure mathematics, astronomy, and physics. From 1687 until 1915, no significant modification of his gravitation theory was made. As refined observations and measurements of the movements of celestial bodies were made, the theories of relativity and quantum mechanics as defined by Albert Einstein evolved. It is now recognized that Newton's laws of motion and attraction not only hold true for bodies in our own galaxy, but also may provide some basis for future research and solution of questions pertaining to the problem of the expanding universe, red-shift, and other extra-galactic phenomena.

THE INFLUENCE OF NEWTON

Shortly following a decline of mathematical studies in England, the important French scholars of the eighteenth century, particularly François Marie Voltaire (1694–1778) became interested in Newton's philosophy. He interested his friend Emilie Marquise du Chatelet-Loment, the important mathematician, in Newton's work, an interest which led to her renowned French translation of the *Principia*. Regarding this publication, Voltaire is said to have declared, "Two wonders have been performed: one that Newton was able to write this work, the other that a woman could translate and explain it." The Collection has the first edition of this translation:

> *Principes Mathématiques de la Philosophie Naturelle,* Par feue Madame la Marquise du Chastellet, Paris, 2 vols., 1759.

As the result of Voltaire's influence, the French scholars of the eighteenth century responded to the new Newtonian concept of gravitation astronomy as the only way to explain the movements of the celestial bodies. Heretofore, Descartes' vortex theory had been used to explain the celestial phenomena. Some of the works of Voltaire which are in the Collection are listed here.

> *The elements of Sir Isaac Newton's philosophy . . . Translated from the French . . .* London, 1738.

> *Elémens de la philosophie de Neuton . . .* Nouv. éd. London, 1738.

> *Elémens de la philosophie de Neuton, mis à la portée de tout le monde . . .* Amsterdam, 1738.

> *Elementi della filosofia del Neuton (!) esposti dal signor di Voltaire; tradotti dal Francese.* Venezia, 1741.

> *Elémens de la philosophie de Neuton. Contenant le métaphysique, la théorie de la lumière, et celle du monde . . .* Nouv. éd. A. Londres, 1745.

🖖 *The metaphysics of Sir Isaac Newton: or, A comparison between the opinions of Sir Isaac Newton and Mr. Leibnitz . . . Translated from the French.* London, 1747.

🖖 *Elémens de philosophie de Newton, divisés en trois parties.* Nouv. éd. Neuchatel. Paris, 1772. ("Eloge historique de Madame la Marquise de Chatelet. 1754": p. 3–16.)

Among the first of the Continental scholars to be awakened to Newtonian astronomy and mathematics was Daniel Bernoulli (1700–1782). He received fame as a Swiss mathematician and physicist, and in 1750 became a professor of physics at the University of Basel. Jacques Bernoulli (1654–1705) improved differential calculus, as invented by Newton and Leibniz, and solved many original problems in celestial mechanics. These two scholars are represented in the Collection by:

🖖 Bernoulli, Daniel. *Recherches physiques et astronomiques sur le problème proposé pour la seconde fois par l'Académie royale des sciences de Paris. Quelle est la cause physique de l'inclinaison des plans des orbites des planètes par rapport au plan de l'équateur de la révolution du soleil autour de son axe; et d'où vient que les inclinaisons de ces orbites sont différentes entre elles.* Pièce de M. Daniel Bernoulli . . . qui a partagé le prix double de l'année 1734. Tr. en français par son auteur. 2 éd. Paris, 1808.

🖖 Bernoulli, Jacques. *The doctrine of permutations and combinations, being an essential and fundamental part of the doctrine of chances; as it is delivered by Mr. James Bernoulli, in his excellent treatise on the doctrine of chances, intitled, Ars conjectandi, and by the celebrated Dr. John Wallis, of Oxford, in a tract intitled from the subject, and published at the end of his treatise on algebra: in the former of which tracts is contained, a demonstration of Sir Isaac Newton's famous binomial theorem, in the cases of integral powers. Together with some other useful mathematical tracts.* London, 1795.

Certainly one of the greatest of the Newtonian scholars in Europe was Leonhard Euler (1707–1783). He was professor of physics in the Academy of Sciences in St. Petersburg and later went to Berlin where he served as a member of the Academy of Sciences for twenty-five years. He returned to Russia in 1766. His great contributions to mathematics and astronomy, as well as to physics, are all well known. Various early editions of his works are in the Collection.

🖖 *Mechanica, sive Motus scientia analytice exposita* . . . Petropoli, 1736.

🖖 *Theoria motuum planetarum et cometarum . . . Una cum calculo, quo cometae, qui annis 1680, et 1681 . . .* Berolini, 1744.

🖖 *L. Euleri Opuscula varii argumenti . . .* Berolini, 1746. 3 v. in 1.

🖖 *Introductio in analysin infinitorum.* Lausanne, 1748.

🖖 *Introductio in analysin infinitorum.* Editio nova. Lugduni, 1797.

Recherches sur le mouvement des corps celestes en general . . . Berlin, 1749.

Theoria motus lunae exhibens omnes eius inaequalitates . . . Berolini, 1753.

Institutiones calculi differentialis cum eius usu in analysi finitorum ac doctrina serierum. Petropolitanae, 1755.

Methodus facilis motus corporum coelestium utcunque perturbatos ad rationem calculi astronomici revocandi . . . St. Petersburg, 1768.

Institutiones calculi integralis; volumen primum-tertium, in quo methodus integrandi a primis principiis usque ad integrationem aequationum differentialium primi gradus pertractatur. Petropoli, 1770–92.

Alexis Claude Clairaut (1713–1765), a French scientist, was famous for both the strength and the extraordinary precocity of his genius. At six years of age he is said to have understood L'Hopital's treatise of infinitesimals. At twelve he read before the Academy of Sciences in Paris a paper on certain curves which he had discovered, and at eighteen he became a member of the Academy. Among his best-known works is his analytical study of "the problem of the three bodies," and the application of its results to the study of the moon and of Halley's comet. The following editions are in the Collection:

Théorie de la figure de la terre, tirée des principes de l'hydrostatique. Paris, 1743.

Theorie de la lune deduite du seul principe de l'attraction reciproquement proportionelle aux quarrés des distances . . . St. Petersbourg, 1752. (This was the essay on which Clairaut won the grand prize of the Imperial Academy of Science at St. Petersburg.) The second edition of this essay was published in Paris, 1765.

Théorie du mouvement des comètes, dans laquelle on a égard aux altérations que leurs orbites éprouvent par l'action des planètes. Paris, 1760.

The most celebrated of all French mathematicians was Joseph Louis Lagrange (1736–1813). He was appointed professor of mathematics at the military school at Turin in 1754 and succeeded Euler as director of the Academy in Berlin in 1766. In 1787 he settled in Paris, where he headed the commission appointed to draw up a system of weights and measures. He made an important and basic contribution to the calculus of variations. The Collection includes editions of two of his works:

Leçons sur le calcul des fonctions . . . Nouv. éd. Paris, 1806.

Méchanique analitique. Paris, 1788. Nouv. éd. Paris, 1811–15. 2 v. in 1.

Pierre Simon Laplace (1749–1827) was known as the Newton of France. His most important researches were those concerned with the inequality of the motions of Jupiter and Saturn, the lunar motions, the probabilities, and the tides. The Collection contains the following works of Laplace:

- *Oeuvres de Laplace* . . . Paris, 1843–47. 7 vols.

- *Elementary illustrations of the Celestial mechanics of Laplace* . . . London, 1821. English edition, London, 1832.

- *Exposition du système du monde* . . . 2e éd., Paris, 1799. Another ed., Bruxelles, 1826.

- *The system of the world* . . . Tr. from the French, and elucidated with explanatory notes by H. H. Harte . . . Dublin, 1830.

Two important scholars concerned with the development of celestial mechanics in France in the nineteenth century should be mentioned here. One was Jules Henri Poincaré (1854–1912). Poincaré became a professor at the Academy of Sciences in Paris in 1881 and continued his work there for most of his life. His work on the theory of functions, especially as applicable to physics, and the measurements of mechanical systems was particularly important. A partial listing of the various editions of his books in the Collection include:

- *Leçons de mécanique céleste professées à la Sorbonne* . . . Paris, 1905–10.

- *Les méthodes nouvelles de la mécanique céleste,* . . . . Paris, 1892–99.

- . . . *Leçons sur les hypothèses cosmogoniques professées à la Sorbonne* . . . Paris, 1911.

Other books that would place him high in the order of the scientific philosophers are two editions of *Science and Hypothesis,* one with a preface by J. Larmor, London, 1905, and the other the authorized translation by George Bruce Halsted, with a special preface by M. Poincaré, and an introduction by Josiah Royce, New York, 1905. Another important contribution is a book entitled *The Value of Science,* translated by Halsted with a special prefatory essay, New York, 1907.

François F. Tisserand (1845–1896) was first an astronomer at the Paris Observatory and later was appointed professor of celestial mechanics at the Sorbonne in 1883. In 1892 he became director of the Paris Observatory. His brilliant writings and research resulted in the publication of two books which are in the Collection:

- *Traité de mécanique céleste* . . . Paris, 1889–96. 4 vols.

- . . . *Leçons de cosmographie.* Joint author, Henri Andoyer. Paris, 1920.

The principal Dutch scientist in the field of celestial mechanics was Christian Huygens (1629–1695). Huygens' most important work was in mathematics and physics, and he was the founder of the wave theory of light. His first scientific work was in mathematics, but he was attracted to improvements in the telescope and the clock as practical problems in aids to navigation. With his brother, Constantijn, he developed (1655) a method of grinding lenses that minimized aberration of light. The new lenses permitted him to resolve Saturn's rings, to discover that planet's sixth satellite, and to investigate other astronomical phenomena. In 1657 he made the first pendulum-regulated clock, and he subsequently investigated the problems of the compound pendulum and the principles of gravity. He discovered the polarization of light and, as an early experimenter and theorist in physics, he stands near Isaac Newton as his younger contemporary. The Collection contains the following volumes:

Opera varia. Lugduni, 1724. 4 v. in 1.

Oeuvres complètes . . . La Haye, 1889–1937. [The Collection contains only volumes 8 (1889), 16 (1929), 18 (1934), and 19 (1937)—volumes which contain much Newton material including correspondence.]

Systema Saturnium, sive, De causis mirandorum Saturni phaenomenon, . . . Hagae, 1659.

Traité de la lumiere où sont expliquées les causes de ce qui luy arrive dans la réflexion et dans la réfraction et particulièrement dans l'étrange réfraction du cristal d'Islande . . . Lipsiae, 1885.

In Germany the most noteworthy achievement was perhaps the development of the infinitesimal calculus of G. G. Leibniz (1646–1716). Leibniz was probably Germany's greatest scientific philosopher. A precocious child, he was learned in Latin and Greek and a student of philosophy before he entered the University of Leipzig at the age of 15. From 1672 to 1676 he was in the diplomatic service and availed himself of the opportunity to discuss philosophy with Descartes' disciple, Malebranche, and mathematics with the scientist, Huygens. During these years he visited England, met Boyle and Newton, and attended meetings of the Royal Society, of which he became a Fellow in 1673. During this period mathematics became his major interest, and it was during the years 1675 to 1676 that he worked out his method of infinitesimal calculus, which, when published in 1684, led to some controversy with Newton who had developed his calculus in 1665. Both had probably discovered the methods of fluxion at the same time. Today, however, credit is given to both men, but Leibniz' designation is probably the most convenient and is more widely used today. The Collection contains:

Oeuvres; nouv. éd., collationnée sur les meilleurs textes, et précédée d'une introd. par M. A. Jacques. Paris, 1846. 2 volumes. "Eloge de M. Leibniz, par M. de Fontenelle": v. 2, p. 1–30.

Virorum celeberr. Got. Gul. Leibnitii et Johan Bernoullii Commer-

cium philosophicum et mathematicum . . . Lausannae, 1745. 2 v. (2 sets).

🔖 *Leibnitz' mathematical correspondence with Newton, Oldenburg, Collins, Vitale Giordino, Hugens van Zulichem, Galloys, & the marquis de L'Hospital* . . . Berlin, 1851.

🔖 *Leibnizens und Huygens' Briefwechsel mit Papin, nebst der Biographie Papin's und einigen zugehörigen Briefen und Actenstücken* . . . Berlin, 1881.

Karl Friedrich Gauss (1777–1855) was the most important German mathematician and astronomer of the following century. Gauss was appointed professor of mathematics at Göttingen, where all his work was accomplished. His principal work, published in 1809, was the *Theoria Motus Corporum Coelestium*. His other works were in the field of earth magnetism and optics.

Contemporary with the French school of celestial mechanics were the Russian scientists. Mikhail V. Lomonosov (c. 1711–1765) was perhaps the greatest Russian scientist of the eighteenth century. In 1730, at the age of nineteen, Lomonosov entered the Slav-Greek-Latin Academy in Moscow. In 1736 he moved to St. Petersburg, where he continued his education at the Academy of Sciences. In the autumn of the same year, Lomonosov was sent to Germany to study mining, where he studied first at the University of Marburg and later at Freiburg. At Marburg he studied natural philosophy with Christian Wolf, a noted German philosopher of that time who also taught astronomy. After his return to St. Petersburg in 1741 Lomonosov continued his astronomical researches and in the summer of 1743 carefully studied the *Philosophiae Naturalis Principia Mathematica* by Isaac Newton. The Collection does not contain any of this scholar's writings, but his work shows the beginning of Newtonian philosophy in Russia.

Clairaut and Euler were both professors at the Academy of Sciences in St. Petersburg and while there they had stimulated the study of celestial mechanics. There was very little Russian activity in the field of celestial mechanics until recently when their most famous modern scholar, A. N. Krylov, translated the *Principia* into the Russian language. His work has been followed by another Russian scholar, Sergei I. Vavilov, who also gave considerable attention to celestial mechanics. In the Collection, there is one title (in Russian) published in 1956 as a memorial to Vavilov which contains all of his scientific papers.

In the United States Newtonian influence began during the Colonial period, which was indeed a most remarkable period in the Newtonian epoch. In 1680 we find a most interesting fact, namely, that direct aid was given to Newton by a series of comet observations made by Thomas Brattle (1657–1713), a graduate of Harvard. These observations were sent to the

Observatory at Greenwich near London, where Flamsteed, the director, communicated them to Halley and Newton, who were then working upon the theory of the gravitational influence of the sun upon the moon and comets, a work which was to result in the *Principia*. Newton expressed his commendation upon the excellent set of observations made by Brattle. A contemporary associate of Brattle's was Thomas Robie (1689–1729), a young tutor at Harvard College, who was greatly interested in astronomy, meteorology, and medicine. As a tutor he evidently instructed the college youth in mathematics and natural philosophy and, in addition, compiled celestial almanacs. These commonplace books bear evidence of his reading and use of Newtonian philosophy.

The Colonial scholars could boast of having fifteen Fellows of the Royal Society in their midst, each with a set of the *Transactions,* and the tutors who came from Cambridge and Oxford were usually equipped with the books which advocated Newton's philosophy, but it is a most puzzling fact that it was not until Robie's lifetime that a copy of the *Principia* was to be found either in the Harvard College Library or in the private libraries of any of the tutors. The absence of this work is noted in the Library's first catalogue of books prepared in 1723 for Thomas Hollis. Copies of Newton's *Opticks* were obtainable, however. It is evident, therefore, that whatever Newtonian philosophy was taught in this country was obtained from secondary sources.

Four of the most outstanding scholars of the Newtonian epoch during the Colonial period were James Logan, John Winthrop, David Rittenhouse, and Cadwallader Colden. Professor Winthrop (1714–1779) graduated from the famous Boston Latin School at the age of fourteen. He established himself as one of Harvard's best students of mathematics. After his graduation in 1732, he retired to his father's home to prepare himself further in mathematics and astronomy. Following Isaac Greenwood's retirement as the first Hollis professor of mathematics and natural philosophy at Harvard, young Winthrop was appointed to the chair at the age of twenty-four and continued to hold the professorship for forty years. Winthrop's best-known works are two lectures on comets, one of which pertains to the return of Halley's comet in 1682. Another undertaking was to observe the transit of Mercury on April 21, 1740, and again when the same phenomenon took place on October 25, 1743. Twenty-six years later he observed the transit of Venus in St. John, New Brunswick, on what was the first astronomical expedition ever sent out from the Colonies. Winthrop is best known as the first Newtonian scholar in America. He possessed the third edition of the *Principia* and his library of scientific books was one of the best in the Colonies. Winthrop was elected a Fellow of the Royal Society in 1766.

At the age of twelve David Rittenhouse (1732–1796) inherited a set of scientific tools and mathematical books, which acquisition led to his becoming an established clockmaker and maker of mathematical instruments in Philadelphia. His mechanical genius was at its zenith in the construction of an improved orrery, now in the possession of the University of Pennsylvania, which was described in the American Philosophical Society *Transactions* in 1771. The transit of Venus, which occurred June 3, 1769, was observed by Rittenhouse with instruments especially designed by himself. His observation concerning this transit is considered to be one of the most accurate and acceptable in the determination of the parallax of the sun. Rittenhouse was elected secretary of the American Philosophical Society in 1771 and succeeded Benjamin Franklin as president in 1791. He was professor of astronomy and vice-provost of the University of Pennsylvania from 1779 to 1782. He was also the first director of the Mint. Rittenhouse was elected an Honorary Fellow of the Royal Society in 1795.

Nathaniel Bowditch (1773–1838) was one of the most remarkable American mathematicians and astronomers. Two of his most important undertakings were the publication in 1802 of *The New American Practical Navigator,* which is probably the most famous work on navigation ever written by an American and his translation with commentary of sections of Laplace's *Mécanique céleste.* The distinguishing feature of Bowditch's work was to clarify Laplace's assumptions.

As we have seen, Newton's influence has been as important in the United States as it was in Europe. Three nineteenth-century mathematicians and astronomers brought the Newtonian epoch in the United States to an interesting and remarkable climax. These outstanding men were: (1) Simon Newcomb (1835–1909), whose principal work extending over many years of research was on the motion of the moon, the perturbations of the moon and its action on the planets, and on other problems relating to the planetary system; (2) George W. Hill (1838–1914), a contemporary of Newcomb's, who associated with him on the same problems in celestial mechanics; and, (3) Ernest W. Brown (1866–1938), an English-trained mathematician from Cambridge who was a great authority on the lunar and planetary theory and constructed one of the most remarkable lunar tables ever made for the use of navigation and observatory work.

In closing this brief sketch of the history of celestial mechanics, mention should be made of the new emphasis which was placed upon Newton's achievements in the Tercentenary Celebration held during July 15–19, 1946, under the auspices of the Royal Society of London and Trinity College, Cambridge, commemorating his life and work. It was probably the most distinguished celebration ever undertaken to honor a scientist.

FREDERICK E. BRASCH

CPSIA information can be obtained
at www.ICGtesting.com
Printed in the USA
BVHW090830070119
537207BV00022B/2778/P